Simon W. France

Spiritual Evolution

How humanity is developed by obedience to inevitable laws. Vol. 1

Simon W. France

Spiritual Evolution
How humanity is developed by obedience to inevitable laws. Vol. 1

ISBN/EAN: 9783337370343

Printed in Europe, USA, Canada, Australia, Japan

Cover: Foto ©Lupo / pixelio.de

More available books at **www.hansebooks.com**

Spiritual Evolution:

How Humanity is Developed by Obedience to Inevitable Laws.

REVISED EDITION
BY S. W. FRANCE

NEW YORK :
1894.

GROWTH AND PROGRESS.

Man's body is but a loom
For weaving the webs of time—
    One, two, three,
    As the case may be.
God's spirit and love are warp and woof,
That make the web at his behoof.

SPIRITUAL EVOLUTION.

INTRODUCTION.

Having lived to the age of maturity, and been compelled to look on the problems of life with my own eyes, as it were, directly, and not through the eyes of others, I have arrived at certain conclusions concerning the nature of man, his destiny and his duty, which appear to me both true and important. Being a member of no Church or religious body, though I have attended various churches from my youth, I am deeply interested in religion, and convinced of the supreme importance of living a true and virtuous life. I am often questioned by my friends about my belief. Hence, I have been led to write out the conclusions which have been forced upon me by thought and experience, hoping thereby at least to make my own position clear, and desiring also, if possible, to make the results of my thought helpful to others.

As I have thought these matters out for myself, with little aid from the speculations of others, amid the labors and trials of a busy life, I have been compelled to present my ideas in my own language, which I have tried to make so simple and plain that all can understand, instead of attempting to use the technical terms of science and philosophy, with which I am not familiar. I make no claim to be a philosopher. The subjects herein discussed have all come before my mind in a practical way, and I have looked upon them as I have been compelled to, with only a sincere desire to find for each problem a practical and rational solution. So I present the matter as I see it. The conclusions to which I have come appear consistent with all my experience; therefore I regard them as true and valid. I do not claim, however, that these conclusions are infallible or perfect in all respects, but hold myself in readiness to change any of them upon evidence that they are erroneous.

GOD IN NATURE.

I am persuaded that there is a God who is the life and source of all the phenomena of the universe. Everything which is the product of his power has temporal life and also a permanent life. Temporal life is sustained by temporal things. The permanent life is God's nature permeating temporal things. Beginning with vegetation, we find that while all

vegetable forms are constantly undergoing processes of growth and decay, there is through all these
processes that power which gives growth and life
from the seed to the stem and the tree, and which,
by continued evolution, makes its way through the
stem and the tree into seed again. Even the processes of decay cannot destroy this life-giving energy.
The products of decayed organisms furnish food for
new growths, and so the forces of life continually
triumph over death, and God is forever manifested
in his creation.

The lower animals are a step higher than vegetation ; they have not only a temporal and permanent
life similar to that which is manifested in vegetable
organisms, but they have also consciousness : as
shown by their actions they possess a light or knowledge which we call instinct. The higher animals
have a brain and a more highly developed organism
and are capable of a higher order of conscious life.
This life is both temporal and permanent in its
character, as is shown by their actions.

Man is a still higher creation than the animals
and has many advantages superior to those of the
brute creation. He has a temporal and permanent
life, as they have, and in addition, the capacity for
developing a moral and a spiritual nature.

Our globe or earth is composed of various elements and forces which contribute to the benefit of all these organizations. The soil furnishes sustenance for vegetation, and vegetation in turn furnishes sustenance for animals. Both these orders of creation furnish sustenance to man. When this process of up-building by the appropriation of sustenance has reached its natural limit, and thus served its purpose, the life departs, and the dust is left to return to the dust. Everything pertaining to these different processes gives evidence that humanity, the animal creation, the vegetable kingdom and the earth itself, and all the materials and forces which constitute it, are governed by certain laws, and that everything on the earth, combined with the earth itself, constitutes one organization, of which there are many in the universe. Man is only one of the subordinate organizations that belong to this earth. Each separate organization has laws to regulate its activities, and which enable it to conform to the requirements of other organizations. God's creation is thus so perfect that it does not require any personal interference or aid from him, other than that which is furnished by his constant presence in these laws and forces which govern it. As far as man's knowledge extends, there is not a spark of evidence that there are any imperfections in God's creation which call for supernatural interference.

The God whom I endeavor to serve is not a person who sits on a distant throne somewhere in the universe, with a sword in his right hand and the Law and Gospel in his left hand, ruling the world like an Oriental despot. As known through his laws, he is a God of love, who bears affection toward all his children, not a part of them only, and who has placed them in this world for a purpose. This purpose is the development of their moral and spiritual natures, and it is accomplished only through laboring for humanity.

God has made men free agents so that they can act out their own desires. This enables them to obey his commands and build up their higher natures, or they can obey the behests of the animal nature and go down. God has so made men that when they do their duty they will absorb from his nature the spiritual elements necessary to build up their own higher life. When they fail to do their duty toward their fellow creatures they will not absorb these spiritual elements, but will lose what have already been appropriated. They will separate themselves from the help of God when they obey the behests of their animal natures by a natural and inevitable law. In so doing, I am persuaded, however, that they do no wrong against God, as is popularly

believed and taught, but rather against their own
natures and their fellow men.

The struggle all through the life of the temporal
man is between the animal nature in him and the
spiritual nature which pertains to the inner or spiritual man. God did not bestow the animal nature
upon man in order to allow him to do a wrong
against the divine nature. He has given man an
animal nature for a good purpose. One of its functions is to aid man in building up the moral nature.
If there were no animal nature to contend with, man
could develop no moral nature. There would be nothing to compel him to do right or good if there were
no animal nature tempting him to an opposite course
of action. The development of the moral nature
would be at a stand-still. The mind would no longer be influenced to direct the temporal man to do a
wrong. Without the animal nature and its temptations there would be no exercise for the moral nature. Those who practice doing right in spite of
these temptations will absorb the divine nature, and
develop the sense of continued obligation to do right,
which we call conscience. The continued practice
of right doing in obedience to the commands of conscience makes right doing a pleasure. When a person possesses this disposition, he has no desire to do

wrong, or to rule over any one else, or to have any one bow down to him or cringe before him. His disposition is rather to do good by serving and helping others. He will not desire to create trouble or cause contention between others. He will desire nothing so much as peace and contentment. If this disposition, as I think, may rightly be regarded as the divine nature acting in man, then there is no evidence that there is any controversy between God and his children. The evidence is just the opposite.

By the phrase "drawing nearer to God," or "drawing away from him," I do not mean to imply, therefore, that we can possibly depart from his presence. I only mean that when we are doing right we partake of his divine nature, but when we are obeying the behests of the animal nature, we cannot thus receive the divine. I am fully persuaded that the divine Being is not only present in our spiritual organism, but that the spiritual organism is through all parts of the temporal body. For that reason, we could not draw near to him nor depart from him, in the ordinary sense of those words, for "in him we live and move and have our being." We can only develop our own spiritual natures by absorbing his nature, or permit them to atrophy by following the behests of our animal inclinations.

GOD IS PERFECT.

What can man say, in the present age, and as a result of his experience, in regard to the existence of a God? Has he any evidence that there is a God? Man learns from experience that there are many things which give evidence by the perfection of their organizations of the existence of some power greater than themselves, which has brought them into existence and sustains them. Everything possesses an organization which appears to be perfectly adapted to the ends for which it was created.

With this evident fact, the traditional story of the fall of Adam does not seem to agree. According to this tradition, God created Adam a pure and perfect being, and gave him Eve for a help-mate. She was tempted by the serpent to eat the forbidden fruit, and in turn induced Adam to eat. By this act, he transgressed the law or commandment of God, and became a sinner. His posterity inherit his sinful nature and partake in his transgressions After many generations, Christ came to redeem the descendants of Adam from the sins with which he had burdened them.

This story seems to me irrational, because if God's

creatures are perfect, Adam and Eve could have had no inclination to sin. The story of the fall implies imperfection in what God had created. My conclusion is that Adam was not created a perfect being, but a being capable, through his own efforts, of self-improvement and development. Therefore, Adam could not fall from a perfect state. Suffering was never entailed on posterity in the way indicated by this tradition, and therefore the belief in Christ's vicarious suffering for the sins of humanity can have no such foundation.

God has created man and endowed him with such faculties that he can take his choice between right and wrong doing. The consequences of the latter choice are evil and suffering, and by means of this he is taught and compelled to do right. God speaks to man through the nature which he has given him, and says "If you will do what is right and labor to build up your higher nature, I will give you of my nature and you can gradually become part of me. But if you will not labor to build up your moral and spiritual nature, you cannot absorb from me and you will go down." God says to man, "I have put you in possession of everything that is necessary to enable you to build up your higher nature: now take your choice between these good and evil paths." God

never withdraws himself from man : he is willing
and ready at all times to help man, if man will only
help himself, and do his duty to his fellow creatures.
Man is born into this world with the capacity to elevate himself by doing right and serving humanity;
or, he can obey the propensities of his animal nature
and in time lose the capacity for self-improvement.
This is all the truth that I can perceive in the story
of the fall.

GOD IS SO FAR AWAY, AND YET SO NEAR.

I can find no evidence that there is any direct
communication from God to man, outside the chan-
nels of man's natural faculties for acquiring knowledge ; nor is there any evidence that there has ever
been any communication from God to man except
through the divine nature that is in man, and constitutes a part of his being. Apparently all that
man knows outside of what is developed by or
through God' nature in him, is but an education—a
wholly natural process. If we take the building up
of humanity for our guide, and test our actions by
that instead of by an assumed supernatural revela-
tion, we have something to rely upon about which
we have some knowledge. This enables man to find
out what his duty is toward his neighbor, and in

serving him he is rendering the truest service to God.

THE TEMPORAL AND SPIRITUAL BODIES.

Man as we see and know him is made up of a body, or physical organism, and a spiritual organism, which is the seat of the intellectual life. The first is subject to the law of waste, repair and decay. It has its beginning and end in time, and therefore I call it the Temporal Man. The second contains powers and capacities which are not limited by temporal or physical conditions, and I therefore term it the inner or Spiritual Man.

The temporal man when in health is a very perfect physical machine—an organization of parts working together harmoniously like the wheels of a watch. Each part has a bearing on the other parts to which it is related. His various powers are all designed to produce certain definite results. We find the condition of the temporal man most perfectly illustrated in the young child. Such a child is, I might say, only an animal, and is more helpless even than a young animal. Yet he has within him the germ or seed of a spiritual organism. When that begins to develop, it absorbs life from the infi-

nite spirit, which is God's spirit, as the physical organism absorbs life from the material world. Thus
the spiritual body is developed, inheriting the qualities of an immortal being, as the temporal man in-
herits those of mortality.

THE ORDER OF DEVELOPMENT.

The Mind and Intellectual Qualities are first developed in and grow with the spiritual body. Little
by little, the personality of the child—the inner man
—develops. It learns to know its parents, its broth-
ers and sisters, the familiar objects by which it is
surrounded. When sufficiently mature, it is taught
the alphabet, and learns to read, to spell, and to acquire a knowledge of the ordinary and special in-
dustries.

The moral qualities of the child are next developed. The child cannot build them up until he has
some instruction and learns to understand something
about right and wrong. The moral qualities develop
later than but in harmony with the intellectual qualities: the two then grow along together side by side.
By the aid of both—the moral qualities and the mind
or intellect—the child or older person is enabled to
decide what he considers right and what wrong. In
the beginning the judgment of the parents takes the

place of the moral sense in the child's mind. The moral qualities are not born in the child, though the germ of his moral sense exists at birth in his spiritual organism: they are first implanted by the parents, and grow until the child can form its own ideas of right and wrong, and act independently of the instructions of others. If the child was not first instructed by the parents, it would know nothing about the moral qualities. After the inner man learns to perceive the difference between right and wrong, and to do the right, the moral nature, as a result of this practice, will gradually grow stronger. This nature will influence the mind, and through it guide the actions of the temporal man, and restrain the animal impulses.

Next to the moral, come the spiritual qualities. After the growth of the moral nature has developed the disposition to do right, or to restrain one's self from the tendency to actions that are positively evil, the further development of the same nature apparently creates the disposition to do good—to actively help the world and our fellow men. This is what I mean by the spiritual nature: that disposition that will not permit the person to rest in a condition of mere negative goodness, but which impels him to love the good and seek to positively benefit and bless his fellow men. This is the disposition which Christ manifested, and so beautifully illustrated in his personal acts while here on earth.

INSPIRATION.

The ordinary view of inspiration is that it is a special or miraculous gift to a few, whereby God directly communicates his will to them. My own view is that instead of being supernatural and occasional in its manifestation, it is natural and universal. God has so created man that he is capable of inspiring and being inspired. I am persuaded that man possesses from the beginning all the faculties and powers which are necessary for him, enabling him to develop light or knowledge by his own efforts. I would define inspiration as light or knowledge transmitted from parent to child or from one person to another. This is brought about in several ways. Man receives impressions from the outer world through the senses of seeing and hearing. Then he is prepared to receive the inspiration which will interpret these impressions to him, and it may come either through these senses or by his own reflection and reasoning concerning the nature of the impressions. One who thus inspires a child, can only convey to him information as far as he himself is

educated or inspired; beyond that he has no power
to inspire. One cannot inspire in others an understanding of that concerning which he himself is ig-
norant.

Consciousness in man, in this sense, is an inspiration, and is that power or quality in man which enables him to know whatever is developed within the
range of his mental faculties. Conscience is also an
inspiration which impels man to know and to manifest the decision of his moral qualities.

That the perception of an object is quite distinct
from the inspiration which gives a person a knowledge or consciousness of its nature and qualities is
readily seen upon reflection. When a person receives an impression on his intellect from the outer
world, this alone does not give him knowledge as to
its true character; but if some person informs him
what it is, the knowledge is conveyed to him through
his senses and is the inspiration of the person to
him. This inspiration unites with the consciousness
of the impression and he then becomes conscious of
what the impression really is.

Again, a person may receive a similar inspiration
through the sense of vision by reading. If I discover a plant which I have never seen before, I may by
searching in a botanical text-book find it there de-

scribed, learn its qualities and attributes and also its name. Or, on the other hand, I may obtain knowledge in similar cases through my own investigation, study and experience. This information comes from the inner man, and is also a genuine inspiration.

The impression of the object on the intellect may be made either before or after the inspiration of the knowledge or consciousness is developed. When the inspiration comes first, then the union with the perception at once produces knowledge or consciousness. When the perception precedes the inspiration, the child or person will carefully observe the new object until it has a perfect impression of it. Then it is ready to receive the inspiration ; that is, the knowledge and consciousness of the real nature of the object.

If God really inspired man directly in any way, man would have an impression on his intellect of the inspiration or knowledge, which he would attribute to its proper source. Experience tells me, however, that I have no such impressions. Except those inspirations that man develops within himself by the natural action of his faculties, or which he receives from others through the senses of seeing or hearing, man has no other modes of acquiring knowledge, except through the impressions made upon

his intellect by the outer world. This shows that all
knowledges, inspirations and developments in consciousness belong to man exclusively, and are in no
sense miraculous or supernatural.

By saying that they belong to man exclusively,
however, I do not wish to be understood as denying
the dependence of man and all his faculties and
powers upon the Deity. The God whom I recognize
and serve, is not found in occasional and miraculous
interferences with the order of nature, but is imme-
diately present in that order everywhere. God is in
nature, including the nature and faculties of man,
whereby he is rendered capable of receiving these inspirations. The air, by means of which we communicate vocal sounds to the ears of others, the voice and
organs of speech, the constitution of the mind and the
brain which enables us to think the thoughts we ut-
ter, and to understand the thoughts of others, are all
evidences of the immediate presence of God in nature. He is, therefore, the common ground of all
communication between persons, the medium of all
inspiration, rather than the author of occasional.
special and supernatural messages to man.

THE MIND.

It will be observed that I not only make a distinc-
tion between the temporal man and the inner or

spiritual man, but I also distinguish between the spiritual man and the mind and between the mind itself, or the consciousness, and the moral, intellectual and spiritual qualities. Our knowledge belongs to the inner or spiritual man, and I am persuaded that it is not generated out of anything temporal, but is constituted out of spiritual things—out of something more than the body and its relations to the material world. If the intellect and mind of man were temporal, the intellectual qualities, and the knowledge gained during life would leave no permanent result. All our mental acquisitions would be a blank after the death of the physical body. The temporal man does not produce or generate anything that is new. Each organ or part of the temporal man has a certain function to perform, and that is all. It operates as a machine and obeys the guidance of the inner man. The mind is developed by the contact of the inner man with the surrounding universe, and it is so constituted that by the aid and action of the brain and bodily organs, the inner man, or child, receives the power and develops the functions necessary to thought and action.

THE INTELLECTUAL QUALITIES.

As soon as the mind, or inner man, and the temporal man, have together gained strength and developed their several functions, they are then prepared to manifest the various intellectual qualities. By intellectual qualities, I mean that part or function of the inner or spiritual man which lies next to and corresponds with the brain in the bodily organism. They are a part, as it were, of the spiritual organism, and constitute the material which the mind uses in the processes of thought. They receive and register the impressions made upon the inner man through the action of the five senses, and store up these impressions for the use of the mind in thinking.

There are three principal grades of the intellectual qualities. The first grade is developed through the sense of sight. When a young child first sees an object, the image of the object is conveyed to the corresponding intellectual quality by the organ of vision. Impressions are thus made and stored up in the quality. After such impressions are made, however, the child does not know what the image is, or what it represents, until it is taught. The parents must teach the child by the use of the voice what the objects are which they see. This additional knowledge is conveyed to the intellectual qualities through the organ of hearing. This will explain the impressions made through the organs of vision. The child will then know what the image is which it sees. When the child is able to read, and to understand what it reads, the same result is attained by and through the organs of vision. For example: when the child sees some new object, something which it has never seen before and knows nothing about, the image will be conveyed to the intellectual qualities, and an impression made thereon. The child will not know what the object is, but if the parents will write the required explanation on paper, and give it to the child to read, the knowledge will then be conveyed to the intellect by the organ of vision, as it was in our first example by the organ of hearing.

The second grade of the intellectual qualities is nnfolded as follows : when the child hears a voice or other sound the impression is directly conveyed to the mind through the organ of hearing. This sound, of itself, does not make any impression on the intellectual qualities, unless it is a new sound. But when the voice or sound conveys knowledge, then the intellectual qualities receive the knowledge thus conveyed, and the mind, by fixing its attention upon them, becomes conscious of the information thus given. This faculty of attention, whereby the mind is enabled to recall past impressions made through the senses on the intellectual qualities, I call the Mind's Eye, since it performs for the mind or consciousness a similar function to that which is performed for the temporal man by the organ of vision. There is this difference, however, in the action of the physical and mental faculties of vision : the natural eye ranges over a wide field of vision, and receives a great many impressions, or impressions from a great many objects at once; while the Mind's Eye, in order to bring to view a past impression made upon the intellectual qualities, must concentrate itself upon that single impression alone, excluding, so far as possible, all others. To the degree in which this concentration is completely effected, the object is perfectly recalled.

Thus, in developing the second grade of the intellectual qualities, if the voice or sound received is new to the child it will have to be taught what it is. When taught by the voice, the knowledge will be conveyed by the organ of hearing to the intellectual quality, where it will be duly established. When the child can read, the knowledge can be conveyed by the organ of vision. The organ of hearing, unlike that of vision, thus conveys knowledge directly to the intellect, and does not require the aid of any other organ to produce the required impression.

The third grade of intellectual qualities is developed by the direct action of the mind, through a process of continuous or concentrated thought. In other words, the Mind's Eye is consciously seeking what it wishes to develop. This involves the activity of those mental faculties commonly known as attention, concentration and memory. When the quality sought by the Mind's Eye is formulated and clearly brought before the mental vision, it will be duly unfolded and established so that it can at any time be brought before the mind.

The faculties of taste, smell and touch differ materially from those of vision and hearing, in the manner in which they convey knowledge to the mind. They construct no image, voice or sound, by means of which they produce impressions on the intellectual qualities. They cannot, therefore, convey knowledge to these qualities until they have first been unfolded by the action of the other senses. After they are thus unfolded or developed, the organs of taste, smell and touch can convey the knowledge which they derive from the outer world to the intellect. For example: when a child tastes something which it has never tasted before, it does not recognize what it is. The parent will have to teach the child with what particular object the peculiar taste is connected. This he does by telling the child; and thus through the organ of hearing the knowledge is conveyed to the intellectual qualities. Later on, the same result is effected through the organ of vision, as before described.

As soon as the child is sufficiently mature to unfold the intellectual qualities, the process of development commences. Impressions will be made slowly at first, but later on with greater frequency. Many impressions will be made of which the child will at first have no true knowledge. As soon as one definite impression is made, the Mind's Eye can seek it out and rest upon it, bringing it thus directly before the mind for examination. Two impressions increase the field of mental vision, and so on. As the child develops with maturer years the impressions are more numerous and more quickly made. The impressions upon the young child, though more slowly made, are apparently more deeply implanted. In later years, when the child is further advanced and better prepared to unfold a higher grade of intellectual qualities, the mind will be called upon for severer labor. It will have to unfold the higher qualities of the intellect, not by the direct action of voice, sound or image, but by submitting the materials thus acquired by past experience, to the Mind's Eye, to be formulated in words or knowledge.

The child first learns the alphabet, observing each
particular letter as it observes other objects, and ob-
taining a knowledge of it as I have before described.
When it begins to formulate these letters into sylla-
bles it will be obliged to develop and use other and
higher qualities. This will require thought and reflection. For example, place before the child the
letters *a* and *b* in the form of a syllable, *ab*. It will
recognise the letters, but it will not know that they
form a syllable or combined sound until it is so
taught. Then, knowing what a syllable is, it will
look carefully at the letters as they are combined,
and reflect upon them until the new impression is
made and the knowledge of the combination is established in the intellectual qualities. As the child
grows and advances, the combinations become more
complex and difficult. After he has formulated some
of the higher qualities of the intellect, and advanced
to a point where he is capable of employing himself
in some industry, or following some special branch
of education; after he has made a success in his
chosen pursuit, he will have learned that the process
of development is an endless one, and he will obtain
some idea of the number of the intellectual qualities
which God has given him to unfold.

FURTHER POINTS CONCERNING THE MIND.

I am convinced that the mind has an existence separate from that of the physical organism. In some respects it is independent of the brain; yet in our earthly life it receives communications from the brain, and acts jointly with it, and also with the intellectual qualities. The mind possesses life; it receives and transmits impressions and is ever active. By reason of its joint activity with the brain, which is a part of the physical organism, it makes use of force in its operations, and requires sustenance and nutrition. It is not sustained, however, by the same means which nourish the physical body, but by other means, required by its higher nature. If the mind were temporal in its nature, it would constitute a part of the physical organism, and be sustained by the same means, and by those only, which sustain the temporal man. If it were temporal, it would be subject to our examination, like the parts of the physical body, and we should know as much about the mind as we do about the brain. I contend, however, that the mind is not temporal, but spiritual. Now, if the mind is spiritual, it must have been developed out of something which is spiritual or lasting. My experience teaches me that the mind, though not itself material, is in close communication with its material organ—the brain. The intellectual qualities are also closely related to the various organs of the brain, and to the mind. What is the structure and appearance, the form and shape of the intellectual qualities, I do not know ; but my experience proves to me that there must be something connected with mind which enables me to remember and recall the objects of my previous observation, or the impressions which they have made, and to picture them before my mental vision.

HOW THE MIND REMEMBERS PAST EVENTS.

I know there is something which receives the impressions and retains the knowledge gained. This knowledge must be located in or on something real and substantial. It cannot be on the physical brain, for all that we could see there, even with the strongest microscope, would be the movements of particles of matter. It cannot be hanging or floating about in the air, without any substantial foundation. Take, for example, a person who has reached a ripe old age : he can recall and see with his Mind's Eye impressions that were made in his early youth. If his mind be clear and his faculties unimpaired, he can see them as perfectly as when the impressions were first made.

The theory that the brain receives the impressions and retains them is no more practical than my own theory, and does not account for all the facts. It would practically leave the spiritual body headless, with no permanent store of wisdom and information, whereas I believe it to be the storehouse of all our knowledge. God teaches us through the observation of creatures living upon the earth that are developed, or transformed, out of lower organizations, as the moth or butterfly from the silk-worm, that each has its proper knowledge developed with it. It is not a special creation, introduced from without, when the transformation takes place, but the knowledge develops, as the form develops, naturally. A similar development of man's spiritual nature takes place during his life upon the earth, and is not, as some suppose, bestowed instantaneously upon him, as a new creation, after the death of the temporal body.

The principles which I have laid down find an illustration in every school-room. Let a teacher have brought before him a class of new pupils, about whom he knows nothing. He will be obliged to study their characters, their modes of action and their dispositions. After they have been under his instruction for some time, and are ready to pass on to a higher grade, he will have the impressions which they have made upon his intellectual faculties deeply implanted, so that when he concentrates his Mind's Eye on one of those pupils, and desires to remember him, he can bring him before his mental or spiritual vision almost as perfectly as if he were present in the body. When he is thus recalling one of his former pupils, he can see no other at the same time. If the impressions were all made directly on the mind itself, he would be able to recall all the pupils at one time, since the impressions were made simultaneously, and are of equal force. If the mind were capable of receiving impressions from all the pupils directly, without the aid of the intellectual qualities, and at the same time, then it would be capable of recalling them at the same time before the mental vision. Experience proves, however, that the Mind's Eye can dwell upon and distinguish only one object at a time. This demonstrates to me that the impressions are not made directly on the mind, and that we must distinguish the intellectual qualities on which they are made both from the mind or consciousness and from the material brain.

Again, when a person takes a journey through a

country which he has never visited before, his eyes
will see many new things, and his ears will hear
new sounds and new voices. Impressions will thus
be taken, and the knowledge so gained will be implanted in the intellectual qualities. After he returns home, at his leisure he will recall the incidents
of his journey. The popular belief seems to be that
when he does so, the Mind's Eye actually revisits
the scenes which it perceives, wandering from place
to place and from object to object. This, however,
is not the case. The mind does not leave the place
where the person now is. The Mind's Eye simply
seeks out those impressions which were made during the journey, upon that part of the inner or spiritual man which I distinguish as the intellectual
qualities.

HOW TO STUDY THE MIND'S ACTION.

We can study this action of the mind most perfectly when all disturbing influences are, so far as
possible, shut out. When I go into a room where
everything is dark and quiet, and concentrate my
Mind's Eye on a village or houses some miles away,
with which I am familiar, the mind apparently goes
directly to the place, but the Mind's Eye does not at
once distinguish any particular object. All that I

am aware of is a vague recollection. If I concentrate my thought on the particular house in which I have dwelt, a change gradually occurs, and the Mind's Eye begins to receive definite impressions of the place. It can see the streets and houses, and can search from house to house until it discovers the particular dwelling with which I am most familiar. If my mind actually went out to those places, as I was educated to think was the case, then I could see other houses and localities as well as the ones with which I am acquainted. Experience teaches me, however, that I cannot see any object with the Mind's Eye unless I first see it with my temporal eyes. This demonstrates to me that the Mind's Eye regards only the impressions previously made on the intellectual qualities. Impressions received through either the organs of vision or of hearing will be located in the direction of the place or places where the objects were when they were originally seen or heard. This still further convinces me that the Mind, the Mind's Eye, and the Intellectual Qualities are not one and the same thing. They are separate. At least the Mind and the Mind's Eye are separate from the Intellectual Qualities, yet they are definitely related to each other, and have communication, one with the other. The impressions made on the intellect through the organs of sense are so located that the Mind's Eye can observe them all in turn, and convey the knowledge thus gained to the mind.

THE MIND AND THE TEMPORAL MAN.

The mind is independent of the temporal man, yet it controls the temporal man as the engineer guides and controls the steam engine. The mind is influenced by the animal in man, and also by his moral nature. In the first instance, it will direct the temporal man to obey the behests of the animal nature. In the second instance, the mind will direct the temporal man to obey the instructions of the moral nature. When the mind is normal, it will not influence the temporal man to do wrong, because it belongs to the inner or spiritual man, and its natural tendencies are toward the good.

The mind's actions when the temporal man is at rest, clearly demonstrate that its existence is separate from that of the physical body. For example: if a person opposes the natural promptings of the mind and makes an effort to prohibit the Mind's Eye from turning from one impression to another, experience teaches us that we cannot do so. Its action is independent of and superior to our volition. Again, when the mind dictates to the temporal man, and commands him to move, how ready he is to obey the command.

HOW THE MEMORY REWARDS AND PUNISHES.

If any person will try the experiment before suggested, of going into a dark room, where all is quiet, and there is nothing to disturb or distract the attention, and if he will direct his Mind's Eye to the good impressions which have been made from time to time by his previous actions, he will find enjoyment in the contemplation. The good deeds which he has inscribed on his book of remembrance will be recalled and be pleasant to look at. On the other hand, if he turns his attention to the evil acts of his past life, he will find them painful to look at. Impressions made years ago will appear as vivid as if made yesterday. In this way, by the action of the mind and its faculties we are continually judged, and rewarded or punished by the experience of pleasure or infliction of pain, according to the nature of our past actions. Every day or hour of quiet contemplation thus becomes a judgment day.

To sum up, therefore, the function of the mind, as I understand it, is to receive and transmit impressions and inspirations on the intellect, to organize them into knowledge, to meditate, to consider, to decide, to dictate, to direct.

The function of the Mind's Eye is to search

through the intellectual qualities, to contemplate the knowledge and images which have been impressed thereon by past experience, and to convey this knowledge to the mind.

The function of the Intellectual Qualities is to receive impressions made by and through the organs of the senses from the outer world, and to store them up for future contemplation.

THE TEMPORAL AND SPIRITUAL BODIES.

I am persuaded that the inner or spiritual man is developed from a seed or germ which is present at birth in the organism of every young child. This germ expands and begins to form the spiritual body as soon as the child begins to grow. The mind, as well as the intellectual, moral and spiritual qualities, are attributes of the spiritual body, and are developed with it. During life, the spiritual man is intimately connected with the temporal man, and guides, preserves and benefits him, as the intellectual qualities are developed.

The outer or temporal body is a perfect organism, composed of different related parts, which in their combination may be compared to a loom or machine for weaving the web of life—or, in other words, for building up the spiritual nature. All right disposi-

tions, the disposition to act rightly, to do good and
to develop knowledge, come from the inner or spiritual man. I am persuaded that anger, the passions
and appetites belong to the temporal man, but dispositions belong to the inner man. The temporal
man also has certain tendencies which belong to its
own nature. This nature, when unduly gratified,
becomes the enemy of man's higher nature. Such
are the angry passions and animal appetites.

The spiritual and temporal bodies are so constructed that they work harmoniously together, acting
upon one another through the organs of sense which
belong to the temporal man. They aid one another,
when properly governed, in their process of growth.
The mind is that particular attribute of the spiritual
man which directs the actions of the temporal man.
The temporal man always obeys the mind's direc-
tions, whether the action of the mind is normal, and
under the influence of the moral and spiritual natures, or whether it is abnormal, and under the influence of the animal nature. The temporal man is
thus obliged to aid in developing the intellectual
qualities. These, in their turn, store up knowledge
which is conveyed to the mind, and thence transmitted through the voice, or otherwise, to direct the actions of the temporal man.

The temporal man also aids in building up the moral qualities. The temporal man is an organism composed of various parts: so also is the spiritual man. They constitute two distinct organizations, yet it requires the activities of both to perfect either. The temporal man must receive aid from the spiritual man in order to educate himself for the duties of life and secure his maintenance. The spiritual man must receive aid from the temporal man in order to develop the intellectual, moral and spiritual qualities.

THE EVIDENCE OF A SPIRITUAL BODY.

What evidence have we, it may be asked, that we have an inner or spiritual body which forms or develops during the life within the temporal body? God's creation as it is manifested in all forms of organic life, is everywhere seen to be a perfect, economical and harmonious system. If we begin with the lowest plant or animal and follow the line of development up to the spiritual man, we shall find the finger of God pointing out all along the line the method by which everything is brought into being. The different forms of vegetation, the various animals, and the temporal body of man, are all developed from seeds, each after its own kind. All the different parts and organs come forth in the course of the development, and they are perfectly adapted to the performance of their various functions. These parts are not developed separately and serially, one after another, at different times, but all commence to grow and are gradually perfected together. They are all parts of one perfect organism, and have a common life. So, also, the qualities of the inner or spiritual man, including the mind, could not develop unless they were connected with some body or organization in common, that acts in unison and harmony with the temporal body. Experience convinces me that the mind, and the intellectual, moral and spiritual qualities cannot be functions or attributes of the temporal body. If this is so, they must be connected with a spiritual body. It is my belief that this body is growing within us during the entire period of our life, and that while it is connected with the temporal body it attains the complete form, size and appearance which it will manifest when the tenporal body separates from it at death.

The common belief is that the spiritual part of man is the so-called soul, which is immaterial and is developed in the temporal body. When it is separated from the body at death, it is believed that the soul passes on to a higher sphere where God has prepared a spiritual body to receive it. To believe that it is necessary for God to separately create such a body in the spiritual world apart from the earthly man, is to limit and underestimate the perfection and economy of the divine method in human development. It is not consistent with what we know of the operations of nature to suppose that it is necessary for God to furnish spiritual bodies in advance and keep them on hand to supply the souls as they pass on to the higher life. God says to us through all the operations of nature : Everything comes from a seed. Out of the seed is developed all forms of animal and vegetable life, including the body of man. The same is also to be assumed as true of the spiritual body, with all its noble faculties and powers.

MAN'S ANIMAL NATURE.

I am persuaded that the sources of all the evils that man has to contend with are anger and the bodily passions and appetites—faculties which he possesses in common with the higher animals ; I therefore call them the animal in the temporal man. From its earliest years, the child has these animal propensities, apparently fully developed. The animal part of man is always active, and ready to exercise control over the mind, so as to induce the mind to direct the temporal man to act as it desires. The animal instincts are powerful, and it is only by the firm exercise of the moral nature that they can be restrained. Take, for example, any young child before his moral qualities are developed. His intellectual qualities and his bodily actions will be more or less under control of the animal until the moral nature comes to his relief. There are times, it is true, when the animal propensities are at rest. At such periods the temporal man is also at peace. But whenever circumstances arise which conflict with the animal tendencies they are at once aroused and endeavor to influence the mind to direct the temporal man to do their bidding. As long as the animal has control over the temporal man he does as it directs, and his appetites crave a continuance of this indulgence; but when the animal is restrained, the temporal man is at rest. The animal instincts have a work to perform, in attempting to control the temporal man and thus opposing the moral nature. The moral nature, like all other natures, grows by exercise, and it is only exercised when something opposes it which it has to overcome. Experience and observation teach me that when man controls his anger, his passions and his appetites, he has conquered all the evil influences which beset him. He will find no further temptation to do wrong. When he willingly obeys the commands of his moral nature

the conflict with the animal will cease, and he will
be at rest and peace with the world. The only devil
which besets man is the evil in his animal nature.

THE MORAL AND ANIMAL NATURES.

Experience thus teaches man that there are two
natures or tendencies in him which oppose each
other. One of these is the moral nature, the function of which is to build up his higher manhood.
The other is the animal nature, the function of
which is to debase and destroy it. The controversy
between these two tendencies continues during the
whole of man's temporal life. He must labor continually, doing right, in order to overcome the animal propensities. There is no other method by
which the animal nature can be restrained and
overcome.

HOW LABOR DEVELOPS THE MORAL NATURE.

The physical and spiritual organisms are so constructed and mutually related that they aid each
other and promote each other's development, when
properly exercised. This can only be done by constant striving and active labor. Parents labor in
instructing their children. This instruction can only
develop the intellectual nature of the child effect-

ively when the child co-operates with the parents, and labors to acquire knowledge. After it has obtained an education, it must also work to earn a living. While it is striving for a maintenance, it has to exert itself to develop its moral qualities and to put them into practice. This effort results in developing the moral nature. Then this nature will force him to do right to others, and such activities will develop the higher spiritual nature. Thus we see that work or exercise is required for the development of both the physical and spiritual bodies.

When the child strives to acquire knowledge, it knows that its acquisition is the result of this labor. When it commences to work for a living, it also learns by experience that it is thus able to earn its daily bread, and that it can be done in no other way. Later in life, when the child is prepared to build up the moral qualities, and comes to take an interest in the instruction of its parents, it likewise learns by experience that only by the practice of moral actions can the moral nature be developed. By continual experience in right actions, a disposition will be created to love the right. He will so learn that all his effort has not been in vain. The struggle to do right will at last develop a love of right for its own sake, which is the crowning glory of the moral nature.

CONSCIOUSNESS.

Self-consciousness is not born in the individual, but is an inspiration. When the child is young, before the mind and intellectual qualities are developed, the inner or spiritual man cannot be in any real sense conscious of anything. The temporal man may experience various sensations in his bodily organs, but he is not aware of what produces the various sensations and pains which he experiences. In this stage of development, the temporal body is like the body of an animal, without true knowledge or self-consciousness. Parents who observe a young child carefully will perceive that the inner or spiritual part of its nature becomes conscious only as fast as the intellectual qualities develop. In the process of this development spiritual knowledge is gradually manifested. The child learns to recognize his own nature as a self-conscious individual. The development of each class of the intellectual qualities will be accompanied by the growth of its related spiritual knowledge. To the degree in which the inner or spiritual man is truly educated, it becomes aware that spiritual knowledge is essential to self-consciousnes. This perception brings with it a disposition to develop such knowledge. When the child first begins to perceive what the image or action truly is which has impressed itself upon the intellectual qualities, this perception constitutes the beginning of consciousness in the child. Consciousness begins to develop at the same time that the child commences to receive impressions from the most familiar objects about him, for instance, his mother or his nurse, by or through the organs of sight or hearing. A person, even the most familiar person, as his mother, is at first to him only a movable object When the impressions are so far perfected that he can distinguish between his mother and some other person, he is then conscious that he knows the difference between such persons. This is the first perfected consciousness in the child.

In the course of time, a person, as we say, forgets many things. The impressions made by past experiences upon the intellectual qualities appear to have faded away or dispersed, or the Mind's Eye is not able readily to locate the position of the qualities so it can see them at any required moment. It may be some time before the impression can be found or recalled which contains the matter that has thus disappeared. During the time when the impressions are thus lost, the consciousness thereof is also lost. Just as soon as the Mind's Eye discovers the lost impressions, and the matter sought for is brought before the mind, at that moment the mind becomes conscious of it, and recognizes the fact that it has been couscious of it before. This fully demonstrates that consciousness depends upon the knowledge and comes and goes with it.

MORAL DEVELOPMENT.

When any person is enjoying physical and mental health, and has nothing to unduly disturb or excite him, his condition is said to be normal. In such a condition the temporal man has no temptation to do wrong. If the person is a child, he will play, and enjoy himself with innocent amusements. If a man, he will take pleasure in his daily vocation. He will have peace and contentment until his animal nature is in some way aroused. Just as soon as the temporal man performs any act that conflicts with the animal propensities, the influence of the animal nature will be felt throughout the entire system of the temporal man, and the mind will be induced to direct the temporal man to obey the demands of his animal propensities. When the animal nature has exhausted itself, it will cease to exert a controlling influence over the mind and the temporal man, and they will return to their normal condition. This state of things continues until after the moral nature begins to develop in the child.

When the moral nature has to some extent been developed, it constitutes an opposing force to the action of the animal propensities. The moral nature always strives to influence the mind to direct the temporal man in opposition to the commands of his animal nature. If anger, the bodily passions and appetites could be eradicated, the mind would be relieved from all evil influences, and would no longer direct the temporal man to do wrong.

When a parent informs his child that a certain action towards its neighbor is wrong, the warning will cause the child to consider the act carefully, to estimate its effects and subsequent influence, and this course of reflection will establish the parent's instructions, or a knowledge of the wrongfulness of the action, in the intellectual qualities. The moral character of the action is thus developed and recorded for the future guidance of the child. Afterwards the child, if well disposed, will be governed by these instructions, unless it discovers through its own experience and observation that the parent's judgment was at fault. In such a case, the child will make his own decision, contrary to that of the parent. It is the duty of the parent to instruct the child from its earliest years until it is able to discover for itself what is right and what is wrong. Every such instruction will constitute a record for the government of the child's conduct, provided he takes an interest in his parent's counsel, and gives it due heed. If the child obeys and practices these instructions, his moral nature will increase and bring with it the disposition to act according to the decisions of the parent. When the child has become capable of deciding for itself what is right and what is wrong it will no longer depend on its parent's instructions. In order to arrive at this condition of self-knowledge and self-determination, however, it must have a basis to start from. This basis is the moral knowledge which it has gained from the parent's instructions. The experience of the child up to the time when it is able to make its own decisions, will give it the conception of right and wrong, and some idea of what is right and what is wrong.

As soon as a situation arises which requires a decision in regard to the rightness or wrongness of an action, the child will reflect about the matter. The Mind's Eye will run over the previous decisions in similar cases which have been made within the child's experience. The mind will note the bearing of these decisions on the case in hand, and decide the matter accordingly. After such a decision is once made, independently of the parent's instructions, it consti-

tutes one more moral quality for its future use and
guidance. When the decision is once made, either
for right or for wrong, the child abides by it and is
governed by it until it learns better, or its judgment
is corrected by subsequent experience. The moral
nature can only enforce a course of action in accordance with the degree of development in the moral
qualities. When a child does an act in opposition
to the one already recorded, the moral sense indicated by that record will at once say that the act is
wrong. It will so dictate because the parents of the
child have taught it that such an act would be wrong.
It is the decision of the moral judgment, so educated, that tells the child what is wrong.

MORAL AND INTELLECTUAL DEVELOPMENT CONTRASTED.

Philosophers tell us that man's intellectual and religious development have preceded his moral development. According to tradition, each tribe or na-
tion, in the earlier ages, had its own conception of
God. These were the intellectual ages of the world,
when morality was apparently unknown. Perfected
man, as we now find him, has been endowed not only with an intellectual nature, but also a moral and
spiritual nature. His intellect is so fashioned that
he can direct it to forward his development in any

direction. This enables him to choose his own course of action, and naturally leads to many diverse ideas and customs of worship. Underneath all human progress, we find one principle or law of development or evolution There is no binding force, however, which controls the intellectual natures of men and unites them in one infallible religious belief. The human intellect puts forth many theories concerning man's relation to God and to the universe. It is no part of man's intellectual activity, however, to develop his moral and spiritual nature. These are of separate origin and character. When man shall learn to combine the moral with the intellectual development, this will pave the way and open the gate for a more perfect unity of humanity.

Man's intellectual nature is developed by study and reflection ; but his moral nature requires a very different mode of procedure. It is only by the practice of doing right to our fellow man that we can insure the growth of the moral nature. This is first commenced under the influence of instruction. When the child or person thus begins to combine the moral with the intellectual development, it takes the first step toward the formation of a true moral nature. This is possible at any point through life.

The so-called spiritual part of man is but an extension of a morality that is largely negative in its nature, consisting in refraining from doing any wrong or injury to our fellow men, into the sphere of active and positive helpfulness. The spiritual nature, also, can only be developed by practice—by striving to do good to humanity.

The freedom of man's intellectual nature enables him to choose his own course of development, and adapt himself to any pursuit in life which he may desire to follow, and from which he may obtain compensation for his labors. He may labor at his chosen occupation continuously, combining but little of the moral with the intellectual in its pursuit. On the other hand, he may perhaps be chiefly interested in moral development and devote but little time to the intellectual. Each stands on its own merits, each has its own proper exercise, and each will bring its appropriate reward. Even if one attains success in his chosen pursuit by close intellectual application, obtains knowledge and wealth, and surrounds himself with all the comforts and luxuries of life, the contentment will be but partial and temporary. It is the nature of the intellectual part of man never to be satisfied.

On the other hand, if one combines the exercise and development of his moral nature with his intellectual activities, in due proportion, he will gradually develop his moral and spiritual natures, and this gives permanent peace and contentment.

CORRESPONDENCE AND DIFFERENCE BETWEEN MEN AND ANIMALS.

I am persuaded that man's intellectual development in earlier ages was similar to that of the higher animals, differing only in the possession by him of the faculty of articulate speech. These animals are apparently of similar natures and dispositions with primitive or savage men. They have a mind or intellect, as well as memory ; an animal nature with its passions ; the disposition to affection similar to that which a mother shows to her child, and the child to its mother. This is God in nature, working through these natural laws and dispositions. When the anger and passions are at rest, they remain so until some disturbing influence acts upon the animal nature. Under such influences, animals act as men do. The higher animals can to some extent be educated by man. Whether they educate each other, or possess a language by which they can communicate with each other, are questions not yet definitely settled. Nor has man any evidence that animals possess any moral development.

With respect to himself, man is conscious that he possesses a moral nature capable of development. He has a power within which is capable of opposing the anger and passions of the animal nature and restraining them. If the animals possessed this power they would give evidence of its possession by a gradual change in their natures in the direction of moral improvement. No such change, however, is observable. This is evidence that moral development commences with man, and does not belong to the animal creation below man.

There is no hindrance to the complete develop ment of the moral nature in man, except such as arises from the animal propensities. In every branch of his development he must combine moral activities with the intellectual, if he desires to build up his moral nature. He must contemplate moral ends in every act, deciding for himself whether the act is right before he performs it. One who so lives will have a pleasant and contented life. There are those who apparently endeavor to put just enough moral purpose into their actions to carry them through a successful business career without personal dishonor or violation of the law. Such may accumulate riches, enjoy all the comforts of life, and develop certain faculties of their nature by successful use ; but they will find no true peace or contentment.

DEFECTS OF OUR EDUCATIONAL METHODS.

Our present educational methods in civilized lands pay more or less attention to moral and intellectual development, but also fill the mind of the child with unverified theories and theologies, as well as undue regard for the forms and formalities of religious worship This brings about a state of mental confusion in the child which is unable to distinguish the difference between the moral and intellectual factors in his mental training. This has been a serious error in our educational systems, from the earliest historical ages to the present time. If the child was taught the true nature of intellectual and moral development, and how to put them into practice, how much easier and simpler it would be for humanity to improve and live a God-like life.

When, in the order of moral development, the intellectual nature is made to conform to moral ends, it loses its purely intellectual character and conforms to the moral. On the other hand, if the moral man becomes indifferent, his action will cease to have this moral quality and again become purely intellectual. Such is the disposition of these two tendencies throughout life : each has its own sphere of

activity, each grows by use and perishes by disuse.
New impressions are made on the intellect with
every effort to combine the moral with the intellectual in action, and these impressions result in an inspiration of moral consciousness. This inspiration
comes from the inner man.

Experience thus teaches us that God's moral nature in man can only be developed by labor. It also
teaches us that the only road to the higher spiritual
life leads through moral development. Intellectual
theories and theologies, forms and ceremonies of
religious worship, belong exclusively to man's intellectual nature and are of no avail in moral and spiritual culture.

There appears to be no power in the intellectual
part of man to lead us any nearer the higher or moral development than the growth of a moral quality,
or the initiation of moral actions. This is the end
of man's intellectual ability in that direction.

The moral law is recognized by man only as a result of practicing moral acts. That gives him a disposition to do right. Repetition of right actions in-
duces a habit of right action ; and the habit by continued repetition becomes pleasurable. The incen-
tive to this habit comes from the inner or spiritual
man. It does not come from the outer world, or

through the impressions conveyed by the senses to the intellect, as other impressions and inspirations do, but from the inner man by a commanding impulse. Intellectual development, therefore, means and implies a process of education. Moral development implies a process of growth, a feeling and inward experience.

If one who has lived a moral life and developed a moral nature does a wrong to his neighbor, an impression is made upon his intellect which no mere intellectual act of repentance can destroy. As long as he fails to do right, he will have no rest or peace. Only by making satisfactory restitution can he again enjoy satisfaction and contentment.

THE EXPLANATION OF CHRIST'S INFLUENCE.

In the time of Christ, the condition of humanity was such that any moral individual must be affected with a feeling of sympathy and a desire to benefit the human race. Christ's parents were undoubtedly moral people, who early gave him moral instruction. He was thus enabled to combine the moral with the intellectual in action in early life. The moral disposition, which is God's nature in man, gradually grew in him, and he became strong. His interest in humanity led him to devote his life to moral development, and to give but little attention to intellectual culture. I take him to have been one of those apt students who are capable of developing rapidly. His profound moral convictions gave him great strength and sympathy for humanity. His early instruction in morality advanced him beyond all others in the line of moral development. His earnest teaching was not acceptable to the people of that age, and led to controversies which resulted in his crucifixion.

This view of Christ's character and work gives us a clue for the separation of the true from the false in the gospel narratives. That portion of his teaching, as there set forth, which corresponds with his personal acts in behalf of humanity, we may regard as authentic. All the remaining features in the tradition belong to the intellectual part of the narrative, and doubtless contain more or less of error. Doubtless Christ conformed to many of the ideas and practices of his time in which he had but little interest. In some cases this may have been obligatory; in others the natural result of education, and prevalent beliefs. But in any case, such acts and ideas belong wholly to the intellectual nature, and constitute no part of the moral development which was the great feature in his life and work.

CONSCIENCE AND THE MORAL NATURE.

In formulating the moral qualities, the child or person develops knowledge of good and evil and conscience or the moral sense. These become instinctive and are what I term inspirations. A continuous effort to develop the moral qualities and obey their commands will cause a disposition to grow not only to love the right, but to do it. This disposition is God's moral nature in man. Further exercise of this disposition will create a spontaneous desire to do good, and its practice will develop God's spiritual nature in man.

In the development of the moral qualities the mind continually makes use of the intellectual qualities in formulating decisions upon the questions brought before it. Each decision makes a new impression on the intellect. This process at last becomes spontaneous and automatic, resulting in an intuition or inspiration of consciousnes, as well as of conscience. When this is accomplished, the intellectual part of the process is no longer necessary. The moral nature or conscience thereafter responds directly and spontaneously whenever a question arises for its decision.

INTELLECT AND MORALS.

When the parents commence to educate the moral nature of the child, they are consciously working toward this end from the moral side, while the child at first regards the efforts which he makes wholly from the intellectual side. But when the child begins to put in practice what the parents have taught it, it is then consciously working from the moral side. All persons who teach and labor for the right and for humanity, are on the moral side. Those who receive that instruction are on the intellectual side, because it is through their intellectual natures that they at first receive these instructions. This prepares them for labor in carrying such instructions into effect, and labor for the right belongs to the moral side, because it tends to the betterment of humanity.

EXPERIENCE IN MORAL DEVELOPMENT.

Experience is a natural part of man's instruction in right doing. He knows by experience that when he practices right doing, he encourages the building up of a disposition to do right and good. These dispositions grow stronger as they are exercised, and enable the person to overcome the animal propensities, and develop a higher and nobler character.

The more perfectly he succeeds in forming such a character, the fewer are the evil deeds which are stored up in his book of remembrance. Thus his burdens, from day to day, are made less, and his encouragements toward the higher life become greater.

To do right means moral development. To do good means spiritual development. And both the moral and spiritual natures are cultivated by all exertions which tend to build up humanity.

MAN MUST MAKE AN EFFORT.

We must not forget, however, that a positive effort is necessary at every step of the way, in order to secure the development of the moral and spiritual natures. It is only when the eager disposition to gain knowledge begins to develop in the child that he makes real progress in this direction. If a person trusts to chance, and fails to make a positive effort, he cannot succeed, intellectually, morally or spiritually.

MORAL AND SPIRITUAL LAWS.

The law of man's intellectual development comprises two principal factors. One is the receiving of the impressions on the intellect, and the other is the inspiration of knowledge from person to person.

This law is preparatory and suggestive of the law for the development of man's moral and spiritual natures.

The law of man's moral and spiritual development also comprises two principal factors. One is the development of a growing disposition to do right, the other of a growing disposition to do good. These dispositions are only developed by the practice of doing right and good, in all our relations with our fellow men.

The development of the moral and spiritual natures in man, demonstrates two things to my mind : 1st, it gives evidence that there is something still higher and nobler to aspire to beyond the boundaries of this life ; 2d, if this be so, it also indicates that the gradual development commenced in this life does not terminate when the separation from the temporal body takes place. The spiritual organism will still live, and the growth of the moral and spiritual natures will continue. If this is in reality the development of God's nature in man, of which I have no doubt, we already have the assurance in this life that we are a part of the divine nature.

THE PROCESS OF MORAL DEVELOPMENT REVIEWED.

Let us now briefly review and reinforce the principles which have been already laid down.

The temporal man, as we have seen, has a work to do in developing the moral qualities. It furnishes that opposing force which compels an active exercise of the moral nature, and thus enables it to develop and increase in strength. The mind, with the aid of the moral qualities, makes the decision for right or wrong. When a child does a wrong act, and the parent knows it, the parent will say: "You must not do so; that is wrong." In so doing, the parent bestows his standard of morality upon the child. The child absorbs it, or is inspired by it. The moral sense infuses the intellectual qualities, and establishes in them the parent's instructions. In every instance, the parent or person under whose guidance the child is placed, must take the part of the moral sense and instruct the inner man before the child can make an independent decision as to right and wrong. In making such a decision, the mind and moral qualities are in communication, and the decision is the result of their combined activity. As soon as some situation arises which presents the possibility of two different courses of action, the mind will reflect thereon. It will compare, and weigh the arguments, pro and con, and make the decision. The decisions so made constitute our standard of morality. Imperfect as they are, they are our only standard until experience leads us to something better or higher. After decisions are made as above described, and the knowledge thereof is established in the intellectual qualities, they become, as I say, the moral qualities developed. They constitute a guide by following which the child or person may develop a moral nature. If so guided in practice from day to day, the moral nature will gradually increase in strength, and the disposition to do right will control the actions of the temporal man. The greater the strength of the moral nature the greater will be its influence over the mind to direct the temporal man in opposition to wrong doing.

CONSCIENCE AND CONSCIOUSNESS.

Conscience is an inspiration of knowledge concerning what is right, and it is developed by the formation of the moral qualities in right action. Conscience stands in the same relation to moral development that consciousness does to the intellectual development. Consciousness implies intellectual knowledge. Conscience implies moral knowledge.

This indicates that both consciousness and con-science belong exclusively to man, and are parts of his nature.

If God dictated directly to man, from his youth to the end of his life, infallible rules for the guidance of his conduct, by what is called conscience, it would be an easy matter for him to do his duty. If every time man did a wrong to his neighbor, God instant-ly and clearly showed him that it was a wrong, he could go on from step to step through life, receiving guidance from without and never developing the moral quality in his own nature. Experience teach-es us that man does not receive any such infallible guidance from God. It teaches that man must be educated and learn to know what a wrong is before his conscience will impel him to avoid it.

If we take a young child before it has learned from its parents or teachers, or through its own ex-perience what is right or wrong, there is not a shad-ow of evidence that it possesses a conscience. After it has been educated and knows something about the nature of good and evil, it is then prepared to devel-op a conscience.

CONSCIENCE NOT INFALLIBLE.

Theologians speak of conscience as the voice of

God, but it is evident from what we learn from nature's inevitable laws that this is not the fact. If God dictated directly to man by means of an infallible conscience, concerning matters pertaining to man's relations with God, this would be evidence that a wrong thus done would be a sin against God. Experience teaches us, however, that there is no such infallible dictation.

On the other hand, experience also teaches that our conceptions of moral obligation are the result of education ; for we have no knowledge of what is right or wrong until we are educated. When we thus come to know what a wrong is, we have a conscience. This conscience dictates to us whenever we commit a wrong against ourselves or against humanity. This proves that the sphere of conscience relates to the affairs which arise between man and man, and has no reference to the relations between God and man.

Conscience is indeed an inspiration or intuition. It does not come directly from God, however, but through the divine nature which is manifested in human society. It is made known to the individual through self-consciousness, as soon as he has received an impression from a moral quality.

The moral nature always impels man to do right —never to do wrong ; but the dictates of conscience are not infallible. They act only in accordance with the standards of right and wrong which have been established in the mind by education. The general belief appears to be that conscience dictates to us infallibly what is right and what is wrong. All people who have been brought up by moral parents have within them a sense of right and wrong which is called conscience. When they are tempted to do an act which does not agree with their education, or when they see another do such an act, they will say "that is not right." It is their conscience, apparently, that so dictates. This dictation is governed by the want of agreement between the act in question and the standard of right, which is the result of their previous moral education. Conscience, therefore, simply expresses the decision of the moral qualities. The development of the moral qualities results in the acquisition of spiritual knowledge. This spiritual knowledge is the result of an educated conscience. Just so far as the inner man has developed its moral qualities, thus far is the conscience educated. As soon as a child is capable of understanding the instructions of its parents, or the decisions which they make for it as to right and wrong, the moral qualities will begin to develop, and conscience will develop along with the increasing strength of the moral qualities.

INTELLECTUAL AND MORAL MISTAKES.

Intellectually man makes many mistakes. These mistakes cause him pain and sorrow ; the pains thus caused by losses, negligence, sickness, and many other things, impede man's progress. But on the other hand, it is by means of such experiences that he learns how to do better, and avoid suffering in the future. After man has obtained this knowledge and is on the way to prosperity, the pains and sorrows of his past experience will gradually disappear. The memory of them remains, but does not give him any pain. This shows that the purpose of such suffering is educational, and that the pains resulting from our intellectual mistakes are relieved when we have profited by their teaching.

Morally, man also makes many mistakes and does many wrongs. This also brings pain and sorrow. When man does a wrong to his neighbor consciously, experience teaches him that it causes pain and makes him unhappy until he makes amends for the wrong. When he has made satisfactory restitution he feels relieved and is happy. The impressions made by the wrong act still remain, but do not give him any pain. This furnishes evidence that moral evil is the natural result of man's own actions, and the cure can be brought about without asking God's personal aid or interference.

If a man does a wrong to his neighbor and his neighbor should pass away before he had made amends for that wrong, can he find any relief for the pains he has thus brought upon himself? Will prayer or penance or anything which he can do in the way of religious expiation take away that pain? Experience says "No." This furnishes evidence that morality is not a matter between God and man, but between man and his fellow man. If God would wipe away those pains, sorrows and impressions for which man cannot make amends, this would demonstrate his ability and willingness to do for man what he cannot do for himself, but this he does not do.

Again, how often does a man do a wrong to his neighbor unconsciously. Days, weeks, or months, even, may pass away before he becomes conscious of the wrong which he has done. Such wrongs are finally revealed to him by man and not by God. If God communicated directly to man through an infallible conscience, he would have known of the wrong when it was committed. Experience teaches that we have no such infallible way of discovering the wrongs that we commit. This is evidence that moral evil is not a wrong against God, but only against man. Man must be educated and know what a wrong is before conscience will dictate to him what he ought to do. If God dictated directly to man by what is called a conscience, there would be no need of education to discover what a wrong is. There is not a shadow of evidence that a man does a wrong against God, or that God interferes with man's acts. Experience also teaches that man puts burdens on himself by his wrong doing He cannot shift them upon any other person. We have the most positive evidence that man does injure himself mentally, morally and physically, by wrongs committed against himself or his fellow men.

THE TEMPORAL MAN'S POWER AND WILL.

That power in the temporal man which enables him to move and act as he wills, is distributed through all parts of his organism, and responds at all times as the mind directs. This power in the physical organism may be compared to that of steam stored in a boiler under pressure, and lying dormant until required for use. I am persuaded that the power that registers and enforces the commands of the will does not proceed from the inner man. The will's function in human action is in connection with the mind and the muscular organism of the temporal man. The will's activity is always exercised over the power of the temporal man, impelling him to do or not to do as it directs. For example, when the mind instructs the temporal man to go to a certain place at a certain time, he will obey. The word "will" simply expresses his willingness or inclination to obey the mind. The will is not something independent of the mind which guides the actions of the temporal man. When the time comes for him to go, the mind directs the temporal power to move and it moves

Again, let us consider the case of a man who has "lost his mind," as we say,—whose brain, from some cause, is diseased, so that the mind or inner man cannot control its action or that of the physical organism. Otherwise, the man may be in good bodily health. Everything may be normal except the brain, which is the mind's organ. He has power to move from place to place. His condition may be compared to that of a steamboat in mid-stream when the pilot has taken his hand from the wheel. The boat drifts from place to place. No man can calculate its movements or tell where it will land. Just as soon as the pilot resumes his place at the wheel, the order is restored, and the boat moves as he directs. So the temporal man when the brain is diseased has power to move from place to place, without definite purpose, not knowing where he is going or where he will stop. He has nothing to guide or direct him:

As soon as his brain returns to a normal state the mind or inner man will again begin to communicate with it, and to direct what the temporal man shall do. During the time while the temporal man is in this abnormal condition, he has no perceptible will power to direct him. This would indicate that the will belongs exclusively to the mind, and is not connected with the intellectual qualities or any other part of the inner man except through the mind. If it were otherwise, the will would not lose its power so completely during the time when the brain is affected. It would undoubtedly have developed some activity under those circumstances. This convinces me that there is no power attached to the will as a separate entity or faculty independent of the mind. If the will has any power, it is, simply to express and enforce the mind's decisions. · The condition of the temporal man, as above described, also convinces me that the mind or inner man is the power which directs the temporal man to move and act.

MAN'S INTELLECTUAL NATURE.

The intellectual and physical parts of man's nature have their own proper methods of action—their own laws of right and wrong—as well as his moral part. There is no evidence that the intellect will lead man to do wrong unless it is influenced by the animal nature. This indicates that the intellect is a natural endowment of God in nature. When man is in health and has nothing to disturb him, his inclinations are naturally to do right. He follows these inclinations peacefully until something disturbs him which arouses his animal propensities. While these propensities are aroused and active, his temptation to wrong will continue ; but when the animal passions are exhausted, he will return to his normal state wherein his intellectual impulses lead him to do right.

GOD'S NATURE IN MAN.

The development of God's nature in man causes him to put away selfishness, makes the doing of right spontaneous, creates a disposition to love to do right and to reach out to help humanity. It causes him to become sympathetic, develops kindness and the desire to do good. Developed in the intellectual part of man, God's nature not only gives rise to the disposition to acquire knowledge but in other ways to perfect the life of the inner man.

Take, for example, a child who has no knowledge of the meaning of the word "kindness;" but is old enough to be taught. Its parents may then show it by acts and explanations what kindness is. It may then do kindly acts to others because of its disposition to obey the instructions of its parents, though it may know nothing of the state of feeling and inclination which is created by doing acts of kindness. After the quality of kindness has thus been developed, a consciousness of its true nature has also arisen in the child's mind, and he then knows what kindness really is. By practicing kindly acts, a disposition will be developed to love this practice. This disposition is also God's nature in man.

Thus, as the child's nature develops intellectually, God's nature grows within him and creates a disposition that speaks to the child and says, "Seek for knowledge." As he develops morally, God's nature also grows within him and creates a disposition that speaks to the child and says, "Do right to humanity." As he develops spiritually, God's nature likewise grows within him and creates a disposition which says, "Do good to all mankind."

The tendency has been among all nations of the earth toward the uplifting of the race to a common level of moral and spiritual life, toward the steady upbuilding of humanity. Great changes have taken place since the earliest periods known to man in the ways by which the accomplishment of this result has been attempted. At first it was thought necessary to placate God or the gods by worship or ceremonial observances, and thus secure their aid for the improvement of human conditions. But thinking men in early ages learned at last by experience that something more was required of them than mere conformance to formalities. Gradually man has learned to depend less and less on ceremonies and formal worship and more and more on laboring for the welfare of his fellow men. When he first began to perceive this fact, he commenced to combine the moral with the intellectual qualities. In advancing from merely intellectual to moral motives, he learns that intellectual theories and formalities are of no use in moral development. Progress in moral and spiritual evolution gives man greater interest in humanity. At last we have come to see that only by laboring for the welfare of others, can man develop his own moral nature. During the present century, great changes have taken place—particularly during the last fifty years—tending to bring the people of different churches and modes of belief in greater accord. How the walls of separation have crumbled down, and the causes of contention have passed away. How much less importance is placed on theories, forms and formalities in religion, and how much more on moral and spiritual development. People are gradually uniting in obedience to the inevitable moral and spiritual laws. Intellectual development results in a growing diversity of opinion : but moral development gives the same disposition to all who live a moral and spiritual life—the disposition to do that which is right and good to their fellow men. Every man, from his youth up, has to labor. Experiencing the benefit of this labor, he sees how it may be applied to the development of his moral nature by directing it to the benefit of his fellow creatures. This is real experimental religion, and it is my belief that this is the highest form in which the religious sentiment has ever manifested itself.

LIGHT AND LIFE IN MAN.

There are two things which give man more positive evidence that God constitutes the life and light of nature than all others. First, the capacity of man's intellectual nature is much greater than would be necessary merely to supply the demands of his temporal life. He possesses an innumerable number of intellectual qualities which are never developed in this life. This constitutes a promise and a prophecy of further development in the life to come. God's creation, so far as we know, is perfect in every respect. He does not make one thing perfect and another imperfect. He does not give to one part of his creation the opportunity for a full use and development of all parts of its nature and deny this to another part. The light that is undeveloped in this life, therefore, gives assurance to man of opportunities for further development in the life beyond.

Secondly, the evidence of the growth of God's nature in man in the present life is promise that this growth will continue hereafter. There is no evidence that man's higher dispositions, which are God's nature in him, dwindle and decay with the failure of the physical powers. If they were temporal, and had in view only the achievement of temporal ends, they would lessen as the temporal body approaches the end of its existence; for the weaker the temporal body grows, the less sustenance it furnishes for the exercise of its faculties and functions. On the other hand, a man who has lived a true and noble life has evidence as he draws near the end of a ripe old age, that his better dispositions strengthen with the added years. Even if his career should close with a long sickness and steady dwindling of the physical powers, the same thing is true. God's nature continues strong in his higher faculties and dispositions to the end. This shows conclusively that these dispositions do not spring from the temporal body, but from what I have called the spiritual body, or God in nature.

THE DUTY OF MAN.

When God created man and placed him here on earth, it was evidently for some wise purpose. He gave him life, and also the germ or seed of his spiritual nature, out of which develops the spiritual body. God gave him power, and by calling to his aid all the faculties of the inner or spiritual nature he can develop his intellectual, moral and spiritual qualities. God has also made man a free agent, capable of forming judgments for himself, and acting in accordance therewith. Man has been provided with everything necessary wherewith to maintain himself, and perform his duty during life. In return for these beneficent gifts, God wants man to do something for himself—to earn his daily bread, and to build up his intellectual, moral and spiritual qualities. The first is not a matter of choice, but of compulsion. The development of the higher nature is, however, largely a matter of free choice.

BUILDING UP HUMANITY.

In building up humanity man must draw help and inspiration from the Bible or any other history, from man himself, or the spirit of humanity, which is not limited to any single individual or race or sacred book. The first thing for the individual to do is to educate himself and ascertain what is required of him. Then he must put this knowledge in practice in his relations with his fellow creatures. Everything which aids man to build up humanity, is a moral quality in his nature. Every act done by man for the benefit of the race is a moral act. This demonstrates that man builds up his own moral and spiritual nature by striving to uplift and benefit his fellow men.

There is a certain law, therefore, created by God for the upbuilding of humanity. This is the supreme law of right, known as the moral and spiritual law of man's being. It is not only the privilege but the duty of every man to aid in the betterment of the human race, for the reason that it is a fundamental law created by God which impels him to such action, and its neglect or disobedience results in his own injury and loss.

Anything which man draws from the Bible, or any history or department of literature, or from direct contact with men, which will aid him in this service of the race, is from God : and the fact that it does so aid him is sufficient evidence of its divine origin.

I am persuaded that God is infinitely superior to all desires that man should serve him personally by prayer or worship. He wants man to render service to his fellow-creatures ; and in doing his duty toward himself and his fellow men, he renders the truest service to God, and fulfills the end for which he was created.

This service includes obedience to the physical as well as the moral and spiritual laws of his nature ; for it is evident that when he violates any of these laws both the temporal and spiritual bodies are affected. The violation of physical laws results in the decay of the physical powers, and upon these powers, in part, depends our ability to help and serve others. On the other hand, the violation of moral laws reacts in evil effects upon the physical body. This shows beyond a doubt that man is governed by all these laws, for better or worse, and that only by obedience to them all, can he develop the highest capacities of his manhood.

Moral experience teaches man that duty involves a larger view than that of working for his own selfish interests. It teaches him that if he will do his duty toward his neighbor, he must take into consideration his neighbor's interests as well as his own. He must educate himself, and learn what is right between man and man. This he must practice in all his transactions.

THE STORY OF THE FALL OF MAN.

In the first chapter of Genesis we find an account or tradition of the way in which man was created, and of the origin of good and evil.

"God said, let us make man in our own image, after our own likeness. God created man in his own image; in the image of God created he him, male and female created he them. God formed man of the dust of the ground; he breathed into his nostrils the breath of life, and man became a living soul."

This would appear to indicate that God perfected the physical man before he breathed the breath of life into him, or endowed him with his higher spirit. The question is, looking at the story rationally, Did

God create anger, the passions and the appetites in man originally, when he first became a living soul, or was he, as some suppose, created a perfect being, developing the lower instincts only after he ate the forbidden fruit? The former conception seems to me the most reasonable. If the passions and appetites were originally created in man, and with them the capacity for developing the higher intellectual, moral and spiritual faculties to guide and control the animal nature, then God's creation was perfect and the story of Adam's Fall must be regarded as mythical and unreal. There was no height of superior attainment for him to fall from. The experience of the first man could only have been that to which all men are subjected daily; the transgressions of the physical, moral and spiritual laws of his nature, and consequent suffering of the penalty of such transgressions.

On the other hand, if the first man was created perfect, without the animal passions and appetites, the subsequent reception of these animal tendencies might be regarded as a fall. Would this be consistent with what we know of man's nature, and with our conception of God as a perfect being? This idea seems to involve us in a tissue of contradictory and unnatural assumptions.

If Adam fell, as tradition declares, and all posterity inherited his sin, the result of which could only be removed by the suffering and death of Christ, the question arises, what became of all the people who lived between the time of Adam and that of Christ? Can it be possible that they were all lost? And what will become of the people who are living to-day and who have lived since the time of Christ, and who knew nothing of him or the conditions of redemption? The tradition also declares that Christ existed before the world began: yet he did not make his appearance until about nineteen hundred years ago. Was God's creation and plan for human redemption so imperfect that he could not bring Christ into the world earlier, but must needs let all these people go their way to destruction?

CHRIST AS A TEACHER.

How many of Christ's teachings, as given in the New Testament tradition, are correctly reported, we do not know. But we have abundant evidence that following the example of Christ, and exercising all our powers, as he did, in the service of humanity, will develop the moral and spiritual natures in man. This gives to every man the assurance that in doing what is right and good for himself and mankind, he is doing precisely what Christ did for humanity.

We are justified, I think, in regarding Christ as the greatest moral and spiritual teacher which the world has yet seen. There have been many intellectual teachers since his day, who have had but a small proportion of moral and spiritual development as compared with him. There is no evidence that Christ possessed a superior intellectual development. The evidence, in fact, is just the opposite. This gives assurance that the perfection of character does not depend upon mere intellectual attainments. This is not essential to the development of the moral and spiritual natures of man.

CHRIST'S SUFFERINGS.

This view of Christ's influence and example will not permit us to accept the usual theological conception that Christ suffered for the sins of humanity. I am persuaded that his sufferings were sympathetic: they were caused by the sufferings of humanity, which he saw everywhere around him. It gave him pain and sorrow to see and know the misery which existed among the people of that day. Any person who becomes deeply interested in the welfare of humanity and whose whole soul is devoted to moral and spiritual development, as his was, can only realize the nature and depth of his suffering. This deep sympathy with the ills and sufferings of human nature, can only come from the development of the moral and spiritual natures in the service of others.

THE SOURCE OF SPIRITUAL GROWTH.

The soil of the earth consists of various ingredients which have been prepared in nature's laboratory to be absorbed by vegetation, and thus produce the various kinds of plants, trees, grains, grasses, etc., which we see around us. Out of the same soil grow plants of various kinds and textures, some with soft stems, some with hard, and of a wonderful variety of shapes, sizes and specific natures. Each kind absorbs from the soil that particular kind of material which it needs for its own nourishment and growth. In a similar way, as I conceive it, the spirit of God is related to the spiritual nature of man.

SPIRITUAL ABSORPTION.

Vegetation absorbs the sustenance for building up the plant or tree from the soil. After the nutritious elements are absorbed through the roots, they are ready to be assimilated by the various parts of the vegetable organism. It requires no direct supernatural aid to distribute to each part the sustenance which it needs. When food is digested by men or

animals, it is then distributed and absorbed by the
various bodily organs and tissues, according to their
several needs, by a wholly natural process. God does
not interfere with the operations of nature, and personally dictate that so much nourishment shall go to
the muscular tissues, so much to the bones, and so
much to the brain and nerves. The organism is already so constructed that it will make its own selec-
tion, and appropriate to each part according to its
needs, without any such special dictation or interference. So, by his method in creation, God reveals to
us how the processes of growth are carried forward.
As it is in the vegetable and animal worlds, so it
must be in the spiritual nature of man. It cannot
be possible that God should change his whole
method of procedure in supplying the spirit to the
inner man. He does not do this by piece-meal—or
by special acts of supernatural interference. Like
all other processes of growth, spiritual development
takes place naturally, in accordance with the laws of
absorption and supply. The notion of special dictation or interference belittles our idea of the divine
nature. In my judgment, God lives far above this.
His creation is too perfect to need such intervention.
He so demonstrates to us by the operation of his
laws in the physical, vegetable and animal worlds.
My conclusion is, therefore, that man is placed in

this world to work out his own salvation, and that according to his acts will be his reward. Infinite opportunities are spread before him, and in them is promise of eternal progression.

HOW GOD'S NATURE SPEAKS TO MAN.

As man progresses through life, he will discover that the condition necessary for the elevation of himself and the benefit of humanity, is conformity to many inevitable and inviolable laws of nature. There are some of these laws which speak so distinctly to man that their language can hardly be misinterpreted.

1st. The Laws of the Physical Body.

When man permits himself to be controlled by his animal nature and eats and drinks to excess, he transgresses an inevitable law pertaining to his physical body and causes it to decay or become diseased. In experiencing the effects of this transgression, an impression is made on his intellect and an inspiration which renders him conscious of the injurious nature of the act, and of the cause of the transgression. This is what I call the development of an intellectual quality. When the temptation to repeat the act again occurs to him, he will say, "This act will violate the inevitable law of my physical nature. This I must not do."

If man will take an interest in perfecting his physical organism ; if he will study it and acquaint himself with it, and put what he thus learns in practice, he will be assured a healthy body and a pleasant life. These results will .be evidence that he has not violated the inevitable laws of his physical body.

2d. The Laws of the Intellect.

In like manner, any person who will take an interest in studying the laws of his intellectual development, and put them in daily practice, will then be prepared to do his duty through life. This exercise will give him an experience which will give him confidence in his ability to improve his intellectual nature, if he will exert himself to that end. On the other hand, if he takes no interest in developing this part of his nature, it will remain undeveloped.

3rd. The Inevitable Laws pertaining to Intellectual Right and Wrong.

If a man will thus educate himself in heeding the lessons of experience, he will become conscious of the nature of an act which is intellectually right, and also of that which is intellectually wrong. This consciousness and accompanying inspiration will dictate to him, commanding him to do the right and avoid the wrong.

4th. The Inevitable Law pertaining to Moral Development.

In the same way, after the person has developed moral qualities, and the capacity to perform moral actions, conscience will dictate to him when any question of duty arises between himself and his fellow-beings, and tell him which course of action is right and which is wrong, as far as he is educated and enabled properly to appreciate the results of his actions.

The moral and spiritual natures are a growth and speak to man by an inward feeling or disposition. The moral nature thus gives man that feeling or disposition which impels him to resist all wrong-doing and approve all right-doing between man and man.

The spiritual nature gives man the feeling or disposition to do good.

After man has thus learned the nature of these inevitable laws, he will find that they speak to him daily and tell him what he ought and ought not to do. By conforming to what they say, he will experience an assurance that he is living a better and nobler life, and that the satisfaction of living may be his from day to day, and is not something which he needs to hope for and wait for in an unknown future. The inevitable laws of life thus become, as it were, a conscience to man ; they are God in nature dictating to him.

CONCLUSION.

Finally, I would say, as a result of my experience and observation, that the supreme duty imposed upon us by God is to develop the intellectual part of man, and thus prepare for building up the moral and spiritual qualities of his nature. These qualities are the only ones, so far as I can see, that *must* be developed in order to elevate humanity. After we are prepared to build up these qualities, our additional duty is wholly a practical one. We must constantly exercise our moral nature in doing right, and our spiritual nature in doing good. So doing, man will have obeyed the whole law of God, and he may confidently and calmly await the issues of life and death.

www.ingramcontent.com/pod-product-compliance
Lightning Source LLC
Chambersburg PA
CBHW031445270326
41930CB00007B/875